Elf~help for Giving the Gift of You!

Elf-help for Giving the Gift of You!

written by
Anne Calodich Fone

illustrated by
R.W. Alley

ONE
CARING
PLACE

Abbey Press

Text © 2005 by Anne Calodich Fone
Illustrations © 2005 by St. Meinrad Archabbey
Published by One Caring Place
Abbey Press
St. Meinrad, Indiana 47577

Library of Congress Catalog Number
2004117889

ISBN 0-87029-392-3

Printed in the United States of America

Foreword

We are each a gift to the world, wrapped in our own unique packaging. We have countless chances each day to give ourselves away. Some of us may worry that we will be emptied—but God's love is a limitless source. The more that we bless others, the more we will be blessed.

The most important part of giving is giving yourself as part of each gift. Think back on all you've received. Which gifts would you consider most meaningful? Chances are they were not bought in a store but are a part of someone's heart.

Momentary acts on our part can be momentous within others' lives. There is a world of wishes waiting. There is a world of ways to fill them. May this book guide us to new opportunities to offer assistance and encouragement.

As you open this book, may it open your eyes to the many needs around you. As you turn its pages, may it turn you to those you can best give "the gift of yourself."

1.

Listen to life with your heart.
Opportunities abound. Heed
the needs of the unloved, the
ignored, the lonely, the worried,
the hurting. Love lets no need
go unnoticed.

2.

Giving is born in a heart filled with thankfulness. Choose to live with an attitude of constant gratitude by counting the blessings in each day. Rather than exerting efforts to accumulate more, we will be spurred on to share from the abundance we already have.

3.

We are called to be God's hands and feet, God's loving smile—God's breath of love in someone's trial. But never are we forced. Rather, it is a conscious choice to put love into action.

4.

Good intentions are never enough. We connect by making contact, by taking concrete actions. Bring commitment to your living; bring commitment to your giving.

5.

We are all one family—and
yet we may not feel connected.
Let the love we receive from
God, our Father, teach us to
give to our sisters and brothers.
Thus, "heart-connections" will
be formed—and God's plan
will be fulfilled!

6.

Give others a sense of belonging. Stepping out of your comfort zone to converse with a stranger, ease a teen's awkwardness, or introduce a lonely acquaintance to your circle of friends, will leave them feeling enveloped in thoughtfulness. Don't be surprised to find your own discomfort has also disappeared.

7.

Be dependable daily in your dealings with others. When you give your word, keep it. When you make a promise, honor it. Few gifts reassure people more of their value than loyalty, reliability, and simply being there for them.

8.

We cannot give respect without first giving acceptance. Acceptance recognizes and honors our differences. Respect refuses to make assumptions about others; it listens and learns from each person. Both self-worth and dignity flourish when we give acceptance and respect.

9.

Be generous with your smiles and hugs. They cost so little— yet give so much. Smiles are small gestures that offer great warmth and reassurance. Hugs can touch and wrap a heart in love, affection, or comfort. By expressing ourselves more freely, we experience life more fully.

10.

Pay more attention to giving attention. When others need to share, do we listen without interrupting? Are we listening with our heart, not just our head? Are we ignoring all other distractions? Are we offering care and support? Studies show besides giving others an outlet, we may be boosting our own emotional well-being.

11.

When we look for the good within others, good is what we will find. Applaud and build people up by pointing out their best points. Give lists to family and friends of their most endearing qualities. Create of your life a sweet garden of praise! Hand out bouquets daily!

12.

Give a good example to children. Make fun and frequent games of finding and filling new needs. Watch their compassion and character grow as they sponsor a child overseas, bake cookies for shut-ins, donate toys to a hospital, raise money for charity. Follow their lead in creativity and enthusiasm.

13.

Encouragement reminds a
heart that it is not alone.
Your supportive shoulder
camping out in their corner
can help shelter others from
storms. A compassionate ear
and comforting words can build
bridges of sweet understanding.
Following up with cards, phone
calls, or visits will keep that
positive energy flowing.

14.

Do not forget to give to yourself. You cannot give to others from an empty vessel. Scheduling time daily for self and with God keeps you emotionally and spiritually filled. Replenishing your spirit when needed will result in a renewed desire and energy to keep on sharing and giving.

15.

The giving you do always
comes back to you. It is a
supernatural law that the
more you give of yourself, the
richer your life will become.
Sow sweet seeds of giving and
know abundant living!

16.

Give others the truth about yourself. Sometimes sharing our own flaws and failures helps people feel more at ease. We are all human. Admitting our weaknesses can form bonds of great strength while allowing others to share their own vulnerability.

17.

Don't forget your spouse
and children when you give
appreciation. Elevate the efforts
of others with enthusiastic
compliments, sincere notes
of gratitude, heartfelt
commendations to superiors.
Appreciation tells a person,
"What you do is important!"
It can help restore their faith.
It can help renew their spirit.

18.

Give others the benefit of the doubt. We all have bad days; we have all made mistakes. Responding with patience and understanding can help defuse a situation. God's mercies are new every morning. So should ours be with one another.

19.

Don't miss out on sudden chances to give. Keep a special fund ready for others' emergencies. Have you considered buying meal certificates in advance for homeless people you may pass? Can you fit some small toys into your purse to help out a harried mom? Do your best to prepare to be someone's answer to prayer!

20.

Shine your own special sunlight on those out of sight. Bring "home" to the heart of someone homebound with a meal, fresh flowers, a birdfeeder…. Bring hope to the hearts of those hurting in nursing homes, prisons, and hospitals. Seek out brand new ways to brighten a day.

Elf Hollow
Golden Days
- Home -

21.

God gives from a heart pure
and selfless, without obligation,
without expectation. By
following our Creator's unselfish
example, we bring bits of
heaven to earth.

22.

Sometimes, the true privilege of giving may feel more like self-sacrifice. When this happens, try changing your mindset from "give till it hurts" to "give till it helps." This simple shift in thinking can take the focus off you while re-energizing your efforts to reach out to others.

23.

Let go and give laughter. Just as
shared tears tie our heartstrings,
shared laughter tickles them.
The more we loosen up together,
the tighter our bonds become.
Lighten someone's load by
lightening the mood. Share
jokes, humorous stories, and
memories. The joy that you
leave will echo long after.

24.

Give inspiration. While giving advice sparingly, share your own life-lessons lovingly. Hard-earned insights can leave the gifts of faith and hope and peace lingering in lives. Sharing Scriptures, motivational books, and encouraging words that have helped you in the past can bring that same comfort to others.

25.

A specially chosen present makes a soul feel singled out. Take time to question thoughtfully and listen carefully to people's interests and passions. Besides tailoring each gift to "just the right fit," you will find your relationships growing in nature and depth.

26.

A gift for no apparent reason
truly celebrates the person.
Calendars need not dictate
when you give a present.
Any day can be a holiday;
any gift can be "just because."
Who can you surprise today
with a favorite book, a fun
night out, a wish fulfilled?

27.

Anonymous gifts can keep
people guessing—but can't keep
them from receiving—the true
joys of their blessings. Bless
someone who needs it with a
box of groceries, a bag full of
clothes, a basket of toys....
The lack of fanfare you bring
will leave hearts exploding
with gratitude.

28.

In this age of rushing and busyness, giving time says, "You matter to me!" If you're finding it a challenge to arrange dinner with friends, a family game night with your kids, or time to volunteer for a charity, try budgeting your time just like money. Prioritize today. Make a list and make it happen.

29.

Offer hospitality and friendship. A home full of friends fills the heart full of smiles! Set extra places for Saturday breakfast, Sunday brunch, tonight's dinner. Adopt a single mom. Invite that new neighbor or lonely widow for conversation and coffee. Your open-door policy will help unlock hearts.

30.

Take inventory of your strengths to see what talents you can share. Visit a classroom, a pediatric ward, a senior residence…. All can benefit from your experience. Gifts from your kitchen, your garden, or the hobbies you enjoy can also bless others greatly.

31.

Be constantly aware of those who may need prayer. When we ask for help from above, God's faithful hand is called down. Pray, whenever your heart feels prompted, for family, friends, neighbors, community workers, and government leaders. Don't forget those strangers whose needs you hear about in the news.

32.

Sometimes, the giving of love depends more on what is <u>not</u> given. Negativity and criticism have no place in the caring heart. Reject quick judgments in favor of thoughtful responses.

33.

Receiving forgiveness from God reminds us to give it to others. When you refuse to hold grudges and you release the resentment, you, as well, will be freed! Answering a hurt back with love opens the door to peace and to healing.

34.

Love thy neighbor. Your "neighbor" lives across the street; your "neighbor" lives across the world. Volunteer your time, your service, your money to your local church and community, national and international charities. Choose and concentrate on those causes that touch your heart most deeply.

35.

Give others the opportunity to give. Invite schools, libraries, churches, local merchants, and service organizations to run clothing, food, and blood drives. Raise money to pay someone's medical bills. Plant a community garden. Clean up a local playground. Small or large scale, you will all make a difference.

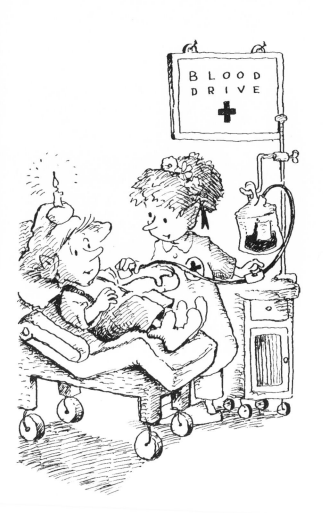

36.

To stay balanced in giving, stay dependent on God. Never saying "no" to needs can leave you feeling burnt out. Ask God to help you decide when and where to serve. You'll find God will equip you for all that you are truly called to give.

37.

Don't let pride or independence stand in the way of others giving to you. Learn to express your needs genuinely and to receive graciously the heart-offerings of others. Receiving brings giving full circle. No gift is truly complete without it.

38.

Don't ever give up on giving.
Despite its many challenges,
giving gives both joy and
purpose to life. Kindness
becomes contagious as it
caresses hearts with caring.
Be a link in a large chain
reaction. Reach out to the
world daily with the unique
gift that is yours!

Anne Calodich Fone is a former elementary and special education teacher who has worked with the physically, mentally, and emotionally challenged. She now works as a full-time freelance writer and considers her writing a ministry of encouragement. Originally from Brooklyn, Anne and her husband, Larry, have raised a daughter, Katie, and now live in upstate New York.

Illustrator for the Abbey Press Elf-help Books, **R.W. Alley** also illustrates and writes children's books. He lives in Barrington, Rhode Island, with his wife, daughter, and son.

The Story of the Abbey Press Elves

The engaging figures that populate the Abbey Press "elf-help" line of publications and products first appeared in 1987 on the pages of a small self-help book called *Be-good-to-yourself Therapy*. Shaped by the publishing staff's vision and defined in R.W. Alley's inventive illustrations, they lived out the author's gentle, self-nurturing advice with charm, poignancy, and humor.

Reader response was so enthusiastic that more Elf-help Books were soon under way, a still-growing series that has inspired a line of related gift products.

The especially endearing character featured in the early books—sporting a cap with a mood-changing candle in its peak—has since been joined by a spirited female elf with flowers in her hair.

These two exuberant, sensitive, resourceful, kindhearted, lovable sprites, along with their lively elfin community, reveal what's truly important as they offer messages of joy and wonder, playfulness and co-creation, wholeness and serenity, the miracle of life and the mystery of God's love.

With wisdom and whimsy, these little creatures with long noses demonstrate the elf-help way to a rich and fulfilling life.

Elf-help Books

...adding "a little character" and a lot
of help to self-help reading!

Gratitude Therapy	#20105
Trust-in-God Therapy	#20119
Elf-help for Overcoming Depression	#20134
New Baby Therapy	#20140
Teacher Therapy	#20145
Stress Therapy	#20153
Making-sense-out-of-suffering Therapy	#20156
Get Well Therapy	#20157
Anger Therapy	#20127
Caregiver Therapy	#20164
Self-esteem Therapy	#20165
Peace Therapy	#20176
Friendship Therapy	#20174
Christmas Therapy (color edition) $5.95	#20175
Happy Birthday Therapy	#20181
Forgiveness Therapy	#20184
Keep-life-simple Therapy	#20185
Celebrate-your-womanhood Therapy	#20189
Acceptance Therapy (color edition) $5.95	#20182

Acceptance Therapy	#20190
Keeping-up-your-spirits Therapy	#20195
Slow-down Therapy	#20203
One-day-at-a-time Therapy	#20204
Prayer Therapy	#20206
Be-good-to-your-marriage Therapy	#20205
Be-good-to-yourself Therapy (hardcover) $10.95	#20196
Be-good-to-yourself Therapy	#20255

Book price is $4.95 unless otherwise noted.
Available at your favorite giftshop or bookstore—
or directly from One Caring Place, Abbey Press
Publications, St. Meinrad, IN 47577.
Or call 1-800-325-2511.
www.carenotes.com